Story in the Snow

Story
in the
Snow

Encounters with the Sasquatch

Lunetta Woods

1997
Galde Press, Inc.
PO Box 460, Lakeville, Minnesota 55044–0460

Story in the Snow
© Copyright 1997 by Lunetta Woods
All rights reserved.
Printed in the United States of America.
No part of this book may be used or reproduced in any
manner whatsoever without written permission from
the publishers except in the case of brief quotations
embodied in critical articles and reviews.

First Edition
First Printing, 1997

Library of Congress Cataloging-in-Publication Data
Woods, Lunetta
    Story in the snow : encounters with the Sasquatch /
Lunetta Woods.
        p.   cm.
    Includes bibliographical references (p. 61)
    1. Sasquatch—Wisconsin.   I. Title.
QL89.2.S2W66   1996
001.9'44—dc20   96–18010
                                                                CIP

Galde Press, Inc.
PO Box 460
Lakeville, Minnesota 55044–0460

Dedication

It is with love and excitement that I dedicate this book to my husband and my sons, who share my dreams. Special thanks to Lone Dancer and Laughing Water, who encouraged and guided me to become a messenger for these special beings.

Forthcoming by Lunetta Woods:

Sequoia: Sasquatch Encounters Continued

Contents

Foreword

THE FAMILY WITH WHOM we have chosen to share our true story lives nestled in the pastoral Wisconsin countryside. The characters are real. However, their names have been changed to protect their anonymity. The exact location must remain a mystery to prevent exploitation of the area where *Story in the Snow* takes place.

This story is an introduction into the heartfelt world of the Sasquatch-Bigfoot. A great deal more remains to be shared with humankind, but this is enough for now.

Open your minds and hearts and read our story. If you believe in angels, you will believe in Sasquatch.

Chapter 1

DOES BIGFOOT SHAPE-SHIFT?" Snow asked herself. She had been running that question through her mind like a broken record ever since a Native American customer of hers brought it up on Friday, December 31, 1993.

If Bigfoots shape-shift, what would they change into? That became the next logical question to Snow's mind. These were not the only thoughts and questions Snow had.

Our relationship with Snow through dreams and through her sense of smell dates back to childhood and beyond. It was years ago, while dating an anthropologist who was in search of Bigfoot, that the idea of Bigfoot living in another dimension was presented. That made a lot of sense to Snow, who had long believed there was much more to this Earth than just the physical domain. At that time, she was told that Bigfoot had the odor of a skunk. It was destined for her to receive those two seeds of truth. It was through her sense of smell that she would know we were present.

Snow was not the only one in her family who could detect when we were with them. Yence, her husband, as well as her two sons Arthur, age ten, and Elden, age seven, could also smell our scent. It became comforting for them to know we were with them. The family not only sensed our scent outside when they were working in the garden or yard, but often when we were with them in the house.

An evening in early March 1994 convinced Yence we were in the same room. Snow and Yence had just crawled into bed when I, Yesoda, a fully grown female Bigfoot, released my scent. It was still winter and the windows were shut, so the chance of it being a skunk was not a possibility. Anyway, skunks hibernate in the winter.

The scent was strong and lingered for some time. Yence and Snow confirmed with each other what they smelled. Though Yence could not see me, he admitted to Snow and himself that something was in the bedroom. Snow knew right away it was me, Yesoda. Snow also understood that I wanted something from her. She had been feeling my gentle tugs increasing in strength for some time.

It was some months earlier, during one of my many visits with Snow, that she gave me my name, Yesoda. It was then when she realized I was one of her guardians.

"Does Bigfoot shape-shift?" Snow asked herself again. Snow told her family about a customer of hers who had brought up the shape-shifting idea.

The whole family was thinking about the magical concept. They already had it in their belief system that Bigfoot exists on another dimension and that we have the ability to come into humankind's dimension whenever we choose to. Still, the idea of Bigfoot shape-shifting entertained their minds at length.

One thing Snow and the boys could do to help them with their new curiosity was to rent a movie involving a family's experiences with a Bigfoot. They thought they could find some more pieces to their Bigfoot puzzle from this new perspective.

It was Thursday, January 5, 1994, around 4:00 P.M. when the snow began to fall, creating a perfect medium for me, Yesoda, to leave some answers. It continued well into the evening, leaving a thick blanket of virgin snow surrounding Snow's house.

The one-hundred-year-old farmhouse stands nestled at the end of a dead-end road in Wisconsin farm country. A large woods forty feet from the house grows to the south.

The family finished watching the movie at 8:00 P.M. Arthur went into the kitchen and turned on the lights that shone on the back yard. He wanted to see how deep the snow was and if it was still falling. More than those two questions were answered.

"Mom! You better come look at this, " Arthur said.

Snow came to the window with Elden close behind. Excitedly, a silent Snow looked out the window.

"There's Bigfoot tracks!" Elden blurted out.

The synchronicity of the movie ending and seeing the tracks in the new-fallen snow led them to believe that their questions were being answered.

From the woods to the south came one set of tracks. They could tell from the window that there was a large space from one footprint to the other, but how much?

They also noticed that each print was placed one in front of the other, forming a straight line.

"I have to go out and look at those tracks more closely," Snow said to the boys.

"We want to come out too," said Arthur and Elden.

Snow started getting on her boots, coat, hat, and gloves.

"No!" Snow said firmly, "I don't want you to upset the tracks, and I need to concentrate on what I'm observing."

The boys were disappointed, but they listened to their mother.

After Snow went out the front door that faced west, the boys ran to the east window, from where they had all seen many sunrises. It was a window that looked out over acres of ideal crop land and hay land, and the same window from which the family had observed many deer, foxes, owls, hawks, and numerous other animals. The story in the snow had begun.

Snow stood outside on the front deck, getting all her warm clothes in place. The night air was very still as the snow kept gently falling. The blanket of snow was already close to a foot deep. The phrase "Winter Wonderland" took on a new meaning as Snow approached the north side of the house.

There, at the top of the brick steps, not more than ten feet from the house, Snow saw deer tracks, many deer tracks one on top of the other, forming sort of a rough circle. One set of tracks led north along the tool shed. This set Snow would follow later.

"Deer tracks," Snow articulated as her flashlight illuminated them. She chose to follow the set of tracks that led east, to the back of the house. Snow became increasingly puzzled as she observed the deer tracks growing larger and larger in size.

When she walked down the hill, she was careful not to disturb the tracks. As she came closer and closer to the line of footprints they had all seen from the kitchen window, Snow stopped in amazement. The human-looking footprints and the varied-sized deer tracks merged. The line of human-looking tracks from the south woods that headed north slowly transformed into deer tracks and then headed west up the hill, where Snow had seen all the tracks forming a circle (see diagram A).

Diagram A

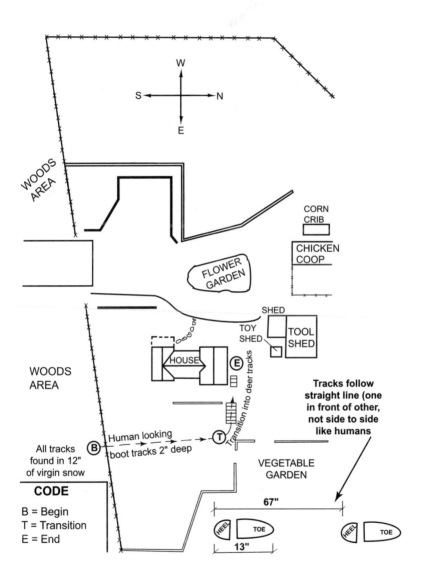

The boys looked out at their mother in her long, white down winter coat. Other than the cone of light from her flashlight, she appeared to be camouflaged by the falling snow.

"What are they, Mom?" Arthur called out from the now open window. The question broke the silence but was soon absorbed by the density of the snow.

"I'm not sure," Snow called to the boys standing there anxiously.

"There are different sized deer tracks leading from the human-looking tracks. Now shut the window! It's too cold to leave it open," Snow said.

It was cold, but Snow wanted what she was observing to be etched in her mind forever.

As she looked at the human-looking tracks, Snow was quick to notice that they only sank about two inches deep into the snow. She sank twelve inches into the snow. Snow also saw that there were two distinct parts to every shallow footprint: The rounded front part of the print, then a space, and then a heel. There was absolutely no spraying of snow behind the heel that happens when humans walk. They were perfect prints, one in front of the other, not side by side, and only two inches deep in the snow. The other very important thing was that they were longer than the size of Snow's eleven-inch boot print, approximately two or three inches longer. The space between each print was the last piece of information to gather.

Snow was in too much of a rush to look for a measuring tape, so she used a rather old-fashioned way of measuring distance. She lined up her heel with the heel of the shallow track and took one-and-one-half giant steps to the heel of the next track. Snow looked at the line of tracks one more time before carefully walking back the same way she had come. The rational part of her mind wanted to explain this all away, but her intuitive side knew the truth.

When she returned to the house but was still outside, Yence came out and measured one-and-one-half of Snow's giant steps, which equaled sixty-seven inches or five-and-one-half feet.

Before entering the front door of her house, Snow stood on the deck and looked into the woods.

"Yesoda, would you please leave more tracks in the snow?" Snow softly asked, feeling (knowing) that she was being watched from another dimension.

Chapter 2

THE NEXT MORNING, Yence and Snow rose around 5:00 A.M. Snow almost always got up with Yence to make his lunch, have a cup of coffee, and chat a bit together before Yence left for work around 5:30 A.M. This morning, they were anxious to look out the eastern kitchen window, not only to see the sunrise like any other morning, but also to find out if Snow's wish had come true. Yence was first to turn the yard light on. "Look outside," he said to Snow, who quickly came to look.

"Oh my God. It looks like there are four or five new sets of tracks," Snow replied.

Yence started making coffee and getting out the bread and other things to make his lunch. Snow had to stare at and study the new tracks for a while. From the window, she noticed new tracks coming from the woods, as well as some leading to the woods. "I'll go out as soon as you leave," she said, taking over the task of making his lunch.

There was more than a foot of snow to deal with and they did not have a garage, so Yence had to dig his truck out. The snowplow had not been up their dead-end road yet, so he barely made it out. Snow watched his headlights disappear down the road and hoped that he would be able to drive the seven miles to work without mishap.

Snow also knew school would get off to a late start or that it would be cancelled, so she put on all her warm clothes. She would wake the boys and make their lunches later, but right now she needed to get outside. Her heart was beating hard with excitement. The idea that her questions about Bigfoot's shape-shifting could be answered by the tracks in the snow was almost unbelievable to her.

On her way to study at least four new sets
of tracks, Snow tried to stay in the same path
she made the night before. She decided to look
at the deer tracks behind the house first. She
now could see much more with the help of the
morning light. Snow studied the line of tracks
made the night before, then a new line of tracks
that also came north from the woods, ending
at a bird feeder at the bottom of the hill. This
set of tracks looked just like the ones made the
night before.

Their length was thirteen inches and they
had the shape of a human footprint with a large
boot on. No toe prints appeared in these tracks.
The new set of tracks was about five feet from
the earlier ones and closer to the house (see
diagram B).

The puzzling thing about this set of tracks
was that the shallow steps led to the bird feeder
and just stopped. Snow walked to the fence line
where the woods began to see if she could spot
any tracks in the woods. From where she stood,
she could not see any similar tracks coming
from inside the woods. The tracks seemed to
have started at the fence line. One set ended
at the feeder, while the set made the previous
night changed size and shape as it reached the
north side of the house.

More questions were going through Snow's mind but she didn't want to stop and try to figure out the story. She had come prepared with a measuring tape and pencil and paper. She determined that the large prints measured thirteen inches long and were five-and-one-half feet apart, just as they had determined the night before. She drew a picture of the footprint and went on to another set of tracks.

This set of tracks headed south along the entire length of the vegetable garden, one in front of the other as before (see diagram C). These were larger prints, seventeen inches long, and not bootlike. There were toe prints in these. Snow crossed the garden fence to follow this set going south to the woods. These also started to change shape, not to a deer print but that of a rabbit.

She once again stood at the fence line and looked into the woods, but farther from the house than before. Snow could see the rabbit tracks go under the fence and enter a large pile of wood and branches.

There was one more set of prints in the back yard that Snow studied before going into the woods. This track also came from the north and led south to the same entrance in the woods (see diagram D). These too were large and had

Diagram B

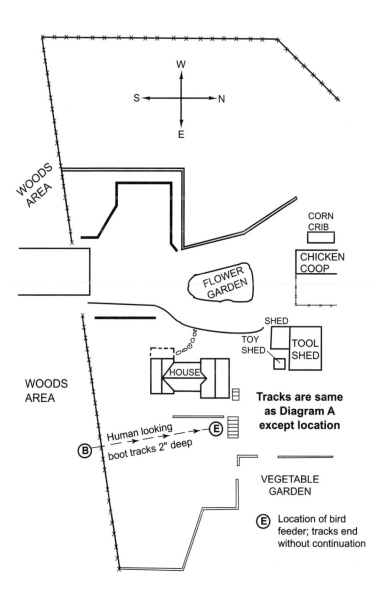

W
S ← → N
E

WOODS AREA

CORN CRIB

CHICKEN COOP

FLOWER GARDEN

SHED
TOY SHED
TOOL SHED

HOUSE

WOODS AREA

Tracks are same as Diagram A except location

Human looking →→ Ⓔ
Ⓑ boot tracks 2" deep

VEGETABLE GARDEN

Ⓔ Location of bird feeder; tracks end without continuation

Diagram C

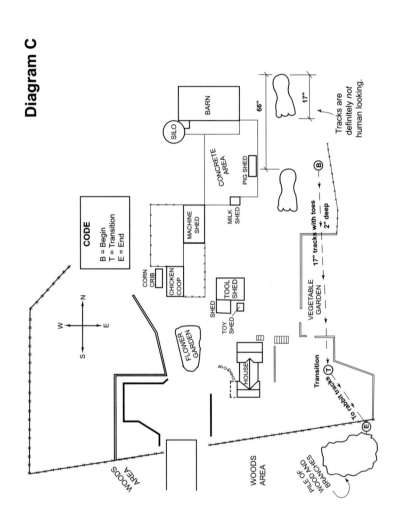

CODE

B = Begin
T = Transition
E = End

BARN

SILO

CONCRETE AREA

PIG SHED

MILK SHED

MACHINE SHED

CORN CRIB

CHICKEN COOP

SHED

TOOL SHED

TOY SHED

HOUSE

FLOWER GARDEN

VEGETABLE GARDEN

WOODS AREA

WOODS AREA

PILE OF WOOD AND BRANCHES

66"

17"

Tracks are definitely *not* human looking.

17" tracks with toes 2" deep

Transition

To rabbit tracks

N
W E
S

Diagram D

CODE

B = Begin
T = Transition
E = End

BARN

SILO

CONCRETE AREA

PIG SHED

MILK SHED

MACHINE SHED

CORN CRIB

CHICKEN COOP

TOOL SHED

SHED

TOY SHED

FLOWER GARDEN

HOUSE

EVERGREEN TREE

VEGETABLE GARDEN

TRACKS ARE SAME AS DIAGRAM C EXCEPT LOCATION.

17-INCH TRACKS APPEAR TO PASS THROUGH TREE

B

T

E

WOODS AREA

WOODS AREA

N
S
W
E

toe prints. The interesting thing about this set was that when they got to a five-foot-high evergreen tree, Snow found a footprint on either side of it.

Snow asked herself how there could be a print on each side of the tree. The only explanation which occurred to her was that we had walked through it. She was right! Beyond the evergreen tree, the tracks changed size and shape, becoming rabbit tracks before entering the woods as before.

Snow was starting to get cold, but she knew she had more tracking to do. As she was about to enter the front door, she looked in front of the house to see if any tracks were left there. From the deck she could see tracks on the driver's side of Yence's little white car. Snow couldn't help running over to look. It was a trail of deer tracks that started in the woods and headed north across the driveway only to stop abruptly at the driver's door of Yence's car. These, like the ones that led to the bird feeder, just stopped (see diagram E).

The woods were calling to her, but she was very cold by now and knew she would have to get the boys ready for the school bus, so she went in. When Snow told the boys about all the new sets of tracks, they too wanted to explore

Diagram E

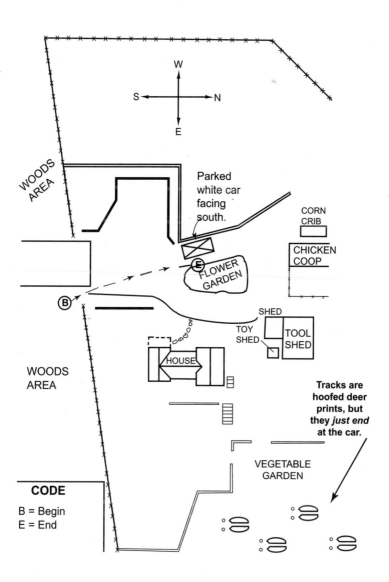

W

S ← → N

E

WOODS AREA

Parked white car facing south.

CORN CRIB

CHICKEN COOP

E FLOWER GARDEN

B

SHED

TOY SHED

TOOL SHED

HOUSE

WOODS AREA

Tracks are hoofed deer prints, but they *just end* at the car.

VEGETABLE GARDEN

CODE

B = Begin
E = End

them. Snow told them that maybe they could do so after school. The boys knew that she wanted more time to study them.

Before getting on the bus, Snow told Arthur and Elden not to say anything to anyone about what they had found. It was hard for them to agree to this. They wanted to tell everyone about the mysterious tracks, but they didn't.

All three of them were outside when the bus came. The snowplow had cleared the road shortly before the bus arrived. Snow knew she would have until 4:00 P.M. to be alone with the messages surrounding her house. After the boys left, she immediately went into the woods in the southeast. She walked close to the fence line, wanting to follow the rabbit tracks that went under the fence leading to the wood pile. She had to walk slowly, because there were many pricker bushes to avoid. Once there, she noticed a piece of fur on the bottom wire. It was dark gray and very soft, just like rabbit fur. She took a plastic bag from her pocket and put the fur in it. Then she continued, following the trail of rabbit tracks that led into the pile of wood and branches (see diagram F).

Snow looked into the large pile from several directions and noticed a new, shallow set of tracks coming from the west side. Unlike any

Diagram F

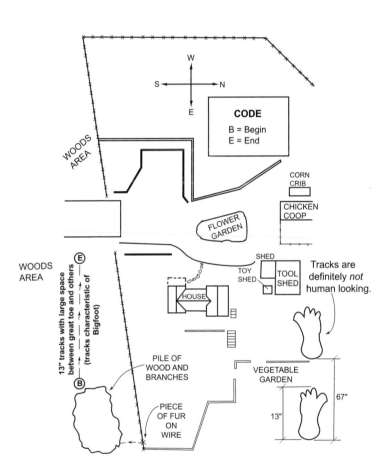

W

S ← → N

E

CODE

B = Begin
E = End

WOODS
AREA

CORN
CRIB

CHICKEN
COOP

FLOWER
GARDEN

SHED

WOODS
AREA

E

TOY
SHED

TOOL
SHED

Tracks are
definitely *not*
human looking.

13" tracks with large space
between great toe and others
(tracks characteristic of
Bigfoot)

HOUSE

B

PILE OF
WOOD AND
BRANCHES

VEGETABLE
GARDEN

67"

PIECE
OF FUR
ON
WIRE

13"

she had seen thus far, they were thirteen inches long with toe marks, but with this set of tracks there was a large space between the first large toe and the others. She drew a diagram and then followed them until they just seemed to end (see diagram F). With pencil and paper in hand and her mind swimming with data, she carefully left the woods. One last set of tracks remained to be studied before she went in and tried to interpret her data. The tracks she wanted to follow led from the many deer tracks on the north side of the house and toward the tool shed.

She walked alongside them, observing the depth of the tracks. All the deer and rabbit tracks had been quite deep in the snow, at a normal depth for an animal in the physical dimension to make.

As she approached the liquid petroleum (L.P.) gas tank on the north side of the tool shed, she ran into a new set of tracks. The deer prints that she was following did not lead into these. These were much different than just their looks. When Snow looked at them, she could feel chills run up and down her spine (see diagram G).

"Reptile," Snow said out loud. The thought of extraterrestrials raced through her mind. These tracks were made up of three talons. The

Diagram G

CODE

B = Begin
E = End

BARN

SILO

CONCRETE AREA

PIG SHED

MACHINE SHED

MILK SHED

CORN CRIB

CHICKEN COOP

SHED

TOOL SHED

TOY SHED

L.P. GAS TANK

Normal deer tracks

FLOWER GARDEN

HOUSE

VEGETABLE GARDEN

WOODS AREA

WOODS AREA

N
W — E
S

REPTILE-EXTRATERRESTRIAL TRACKS

10"

Tracks are definitely not human or animal.

center talon was longer than the ones on either side of it. The tracks appeared as if the being that made them walked side to side, as humans do. The thought of a pheasant went through Snow's mind, but these were too large, about ten inches. These were also very shallow tracks in the deep snow and just seemed to end at another building, the machine shed. There was one other set of tracks that were exactly like these reptilian ones, and these appeared to pace back and forth by the chicken coup.

There had been only wonder, joy, and excitement when Snow had looked at all the tracks, but when she came to these, her blood ran cold.

Sasquatch as drawn by Arthur, age 10

Chapter 3

IT WOULD TAKE UNTIL the following January for Snow to interpret all the tracks left that memorable night. Though many of us dwell in the area where she and her family live, it was only two of us Sasquatch that composed the story in the snow. I, Yesoda, a lifelong companion and guardian to Snow, and Kunta, an adult male Sasquatch. Kunta is a guardian for the whole family, but he mostly watches over the boys, especially Arthur.

We, as a community of Sasquatch, have been observing Snow and her family for years. The story that Kunta and I left in the snow marked the beginning of a more important, intimate relationship with their whole family.

You might ask why we want to communicate with this family. The answer is that we have known Snow since she was a child, and beyond. When she was a small girl, Snow repeatedly dreamed about what she called a gorilla standing outside her bedroom window and looking in while Snow looked out. That being was not a gorilla, but a Sasquatch.

You see, Snow was unlike other children. She was a soul who stored knowledge of us and many other interdimensional beings in her unconscious mind. She used to work with us in days of old, many lifetimes ago. She was a great healer entity who could see the ley lines or gridwork of energy that surrounded the Earth. She could also see the entrances to portals. As a child in this present life, she wandered into portals where we existed.

That is where Snow and I met. We would romp and play with one another. There was a great deal of joy in our time together. For many years, Snow's only memory of our relationship was of a Sasquatch looking into her bedroom window and Snow looking out. All the other memories had to remain in her unconscious mind until she approached the age of forty.

Much information is veiled from human consciousness, but when the time is right, the memories start to filter up from your subconsciousness to your conscious mind.

The days of winter 1994 passed on and all the snow disappeared with the approach of spring, but the story in the snow would remain etched forever in all their minds. Answering Snow's questions led to many more questions. We wanted to communicate with Snow telling her she was right about her interpretations of Bigfoot being able to shape-shift.

To do this, I, Yesoda, came to Snow in an early morning dream. This was the first of many Bigfoot dreams to come in her adult life, but the only one that winter. When Snow went to bed, the Earth was devoid of snow on the ground. Just before waking, Snow dreamed of me. In the dream, she was behind the house facing east, looking at Bigfoot tracks in the snow that lead to the middle of a nine-acre field. At the end of the tracks I stood looking back at Snow while she looked at me. In the dream, she skied, following the tracks toward me, but by the time she arrived at where she saw me standing, I had disappeared. The next morning, after she woke up, she heard Yence call for her. "Snow, come down here and look out the window," Yence said.

It had snowed three inches that night, and there in the snow the prints of both a rabbit and a deer were merged together (see diagram H).

The tracks were only five feet from the house. Yence did not know what to think at first. It was not unusual for a rabbit to come that close to a house, but a deer made him wonder. Snow quickly told Yence about her dream. "Yesoda's letting me know that I'm on course in my understanding of their ability to shape-shift," Snow said excitedly. "Yesoda also wants me to know that she knows I am in pursuit of her," Snow expressed as she recalled the dream.

That would be the last message in the snow and the last time we would come to her in a dream until November 1994.

There were many other forms of communication that needed to be known. Believing that Bigfoot could shape-shift led Snow to her deck of medicine cards. This was a deck of cards consisting of forty-four animals of North America. The Native Americans designed this system of divination to assist humankind on their Earth walk with the animal kingdom. Every animal has its traits, characteristics, and messages to share with the other kingdoms. Snow asked the Great Spirit to guide her to the cards that would represent all the animals we would shape-shift into and communicate through.

Diagram H

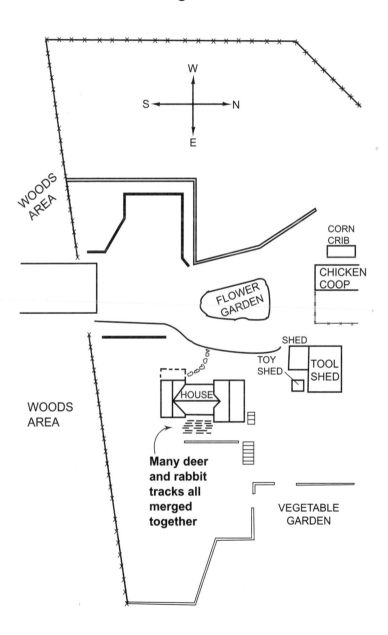

W

S ← → N

E

WOODS
AREA

CORN
CRIB

CHICKEN
COOP

FLOWER
GARDEN

SHED

TOY
SHED

TOOL
SHED

HOUSE

WOODS
AREA

**Many deer
and rabbit
tracks all
merged
together**

VEGETABLE
GARDEN

She placed the deck of cards upside down as instructed and began to select the ones she felt drawn to. Snow drew a total of twelve cards. Each card had a key word for the animal, as shown below:

1. Eagle .... Spirit

2. Hawk .... Messenger

44. Hummingbird . Joy

9. Butterfly ..... Transformation

26. Squirrel ...... Gathering

30. Rabbit .... Fear

25. Fox .... Camouflage

21. Owl .... Deception (Able to see through deception)

4. Deer .... Gentleness

11. Moose .... Self-Esteem

19. Buffalo .... Prayer-Abundance

41. Whale .... Record-Keepers

Throughout the spring and summer of 1994, we came to Snow and her family in many of these forms. One cold day in early spring, Kunta sat on a low branch of a tree in the east as a hawk. Yence and Snow were having their 3:00 P.M. coffee at their kitchen table when Snow saw the hawk. Kunta sat there staring at them through the window. Snow knew this wasn't an ordinary hawk. She went outside and walked slowly toward him.

Kunta sat motionless as Snow walked up to him. He did not express any signs of fear but just looked deep into her soul. They looked at each other for five minutes before Snow went back into the house. It was cold out and she wasn't wearing a coat. She went in to drink hot coffee and watch the hawk from the kitchen table. Kunta stayed for a half-hour more and then flew off.

Many times that summer, I came to Snow's windows as a hummingbird. Snow was keen to note the timing when I appeared. I would come as an affirmation for some kind of action that Snow took in her quest to understand the Bigfoot species better.

Once I came to her window after she had finished writing a letter with a list of questions about us. I came as a hummingbird because there was joy in my heart that she was taking the right steps in collecting the pieces to the Sasquatch puzzle. She understood my visit as a joyous affirmation of her progress.

In the fall, Kunta and I came as a pair of great horned owls. Yence took a day off from work and didn't set the alarm clock the night before. The whole house was still sound asleep at 7:00 A.M. I knew the boys caught the school bus at 7:30 A.M., so we thought we should wake them. Kunta and I started calling to each other outside Snow's bedroom window. Her window was open, so she was quick to hear our morning call. She glanced at the clock and jumped up to wake the boys. Snow correctly believed what happened that sleepy morning was not coincidence.

Another important way in which we communicated with the family was through their sense of smell. One night I came to Snow's bedside and let her know I was there by releasing an odor that you humans would describe as a skunk-like smell.

This was the odor that we would use many times to let the family know we were near. You see, we did not want to appear in our physical forms. We wanted to convey as much information as possible about our species without

creating fear in Snow and her family. Releasing a skunk-like smell that the whole family
could detect became a very comforting experience for them. They began to see and understand the timing with which we let ourselves
be known. By being telepathically in tune with
Snow, we are able to know when she is not
well, if she is full of stress, or if she is on course
with her destiny.

One night Snow went to bed filled with
lots of stress from a day-long trip to Chicago
and back. The driving and the pace of the city
left her feeling tattered and exhausted. I let
her know I was there and concerned about her
well-being. Snow and Yence smelled my pres-
ence. She smiled and held out her hand to me,
thankful for my concern.

Another time not long after that visit I
came once again to her bedside. That night
Snow was worried about the cost of new vitamins, trace minerals, and anti-dioxins she was
directed to take. Not only were they expensive,
but they were hard to swallow. She had to
crush them and drink them with juice to get
them down. Snow was not a pill taker. Concerned, I came to her side, but also to affirm
she was doing the right thing. These pills
would help the energy flow in her body and con-

nect and balance her energies with the Earth. I stayed with her a long time that night, wanting her to know the importance of the vitamins.

Many times when Snow would take her almost daily four-mile walk, I would walk with her. I liked her fast pace and the way she would swing her arms. More importantly it was a good time to channel information to her.

Several times I let myself be known, through her sense of smell, while Snow was driving her car. Sometimes it was just to let her know I was with her to keep her company, but many times it was to encourage her to take action with a train of thought she was having about us.

We often heard her prayers for guidance with all the information that we were giving her. Many times she asked for an affirmation from us. She wanted to make sure she was on course with putting the puzzle together. One way or another, we let her know that she was.

At 5:45 A.M. one morning I visited Snow in her kitchen, through her sense of smell. She wanted to make sure it was me and not Cocoa the dog, who might have been sprayed by a skunk, so she got down on all fours and smelled. Cocoa had her normal doggy odor, so she surmised it was me. Snow said nothing to the boys when she woke them up, but not long afterward, Snow heard Arthur say, "Mom, I smell Yesoda up here."

"I smelled her down here earlier, but I didn't want to say anything," Snow replied.

It made me feel good to know that Arthur's fear about me was fading. I knew that he still feared seeing us in our true Bigfoot form, so we did not materialize. The family's fears and apprehensions about our physical appearance would be removed through a series of dreams.

The morning of February 2, 1995, Snow was hard at work writing in her journal about the experiences she'd had with us. Many of the thoughts and feelings she was writing about us were so true. You see, we chose her to be our spokesperson, our channel, for our true story to be heard in your world. We were happy with her willingness to work with us.

That night at dusk, Freta, another of their dogs, was watching the woods out the window for over an hour. Snow watched Freta's head move back and forth, as if much activity was taking place. Snow looked into the woods where she had seen the footprints coming from the woodpile the year before. She did not see us, but Freta had no trouble seeing us gather, and she was not alarmed. She knew there was

nothing to fear. Snow did sense the massive-
ness of our large bodies, and she was excited to
know that many of us were near.

Snow was getting over a bad cold, so she
was still unable to smell anything. We knew
we could not communicate through her sense
of smell, so we had to chose another sense to
communicate through.

It was dinnertime for Snow and her family.
She had commented about Freta watching the
woods so intently, and that she had sensed lots
of activity there. Just after everyone was set-
tled at the kitchen table, I made a very high-
pitched whistling sound. Arthur and Snow
looked at each other and then to the woods.
Yence said he heard something, but he couldn't
make it out because he has a hearing loss in
one ear. Elden was talking at the time, so he
didn't hear anything.

This was the first time we communicated
with sound. Many of us wanted her to know we
were very pleased with what she wrote about
us that morning. Snow understood the timing
of the affirmation and was thrilled with our
communications with her through the sense of
hearing.

Chapter 4

BEFORE WE STARTED coming to the family in their dreams, it was necessary to guide two wise women, learned in Native American ways, into Snow's path. They would have an important influence, encouraging Snow to take action with the information we were sharing with her.

It was on November 2 when Lone Dancer and Laughing Water came into the Rock Gem and Mineral store where Snow worked. It wasn't long after talking with them when

Snow asked, "Do you have any knowledge about Sasquatch?"

"They are Earth keepers, healers of mother Earth. They only communicate to those who are spiritually rich," Laughing Water said.

"They are communicating to me in the snow and through my sense of smell," Snow said humbly. She went on to explain the questions she had about Bigfoots being able to shape-shift and the tracks that were left in the snow. "I will be writing a book about all the events that are happening," Snow said, somewhat uncertainly.

"You must write the book! There is great urgency with getting this information out! The Sasquatch are depending on you to write their story. If you do not take action, they will have to go to someone else to be their spokesperson," Laughing Water said.

Snow knew Laughing Water was right. "I will start the writing when the snow comes," Snow said, feeling somewhat pressured by what Laughing Water said.

"She will start when the snow comes after the holidays are over," Lone Dancer said, patting Laughing Water on the shoulder and trying to comfort her.

Tears were in Laughing Water's eyes. She was feeling the importance and urgency of this knowledge reaching humankind. The three women knew the survival of the species was in question. They also knew that there was a great deal of fear in people all over the world about us. We knew they would try to kill us out of fear. It was our wish and hope that Snow could help bring enlightenment and understanding about our true nature.

The three women shared addresses and phone numbers. Then they realized that they all lived within five miles of each other, even though the store was forty miles from their homes.

Two weeks later, Lone Dancer and Laughing Water came to Snow's farm to get a sense of the area. Laughing Water was able to see life forms in other dimensions. They both walked the area and told Snow where she first saw the footprints in the snow, and they were correct. Lone Dancer mentioned that they usually exit the back yard and enter the woods exactly where Snow had tracked the prints and found rabbit hair on the fence.

"There are families of Sasquatch who live here; they enjoy your family very much,"

Laughing Water said to Snow as she quietly walked and stood meditatively.

"The next time you see Sasquatch tracks, walk in them," Laughing Water said.

"This will help you connect with them even more," Lone Dancer said.

Laughing Water stood and held on to a wooden fence post that ran parallel to the house.

"This is where a very strong, large Sasquatch stands at night to protect the boys. His name is Kunta and he is their guardian. He keeps watch beneath their bedroom window to protect them from evil that wants to enter," Laughing Water said.

Snow told Laughing Water that Arthur was afraid to go to sleep and would often wake up delirious from nightmares.

Laughing Water told Snow that there were evil forces coming to Arthur when he slept. These evil forces were trying to slow down Snow's mission of writing a book of light and good about Bigfoot. The evil forces knew that her sleep was broken night after night by trying to comfort Arthur. They knew this took much of her energy and filled her with concern and worry. Evil does whatever it can to keep any light worker from doing their work. The three of them left the back yard and walked toward the barn (see diagram I).

"It was over here, between the L.P. gas tank and machine shed where I saw those reptilian tracks," Snow said.

"Snow, you stay here a while. Lone Dancer and I will walk by the barn," Laughing Water said in a firm but gentle voice.

Snow did what she was told and watched from a distance as the two women walked by the silo next to the barn. Snow could see that they were talking to each other with concern as they looked into the silo. They then walked around to the back of the barn and yelled for Snow to come. "This is where they run and play," Lone Dancer said.

"This is where we cross-country ski and go sledding. It does have a very warm, safe feeling, doesn't it?" Snow asked the others.

As the three women walked back to the house, Laughing Water told Snow that she and the boys should stay away from the silo. Of course, Snow wanted to know why. She thought it would have something to do with those reptile-looking tracks. "What did you see in the silo?" Snow asked eagerly.

"I can't tell you at this time," Laughing Water replied.

Snow knew not to push the question any further. They went in to sit in the kitchen and have cake and coffee. The conversation lasted three hours. Many thoughts, feelings, and counsel were shared. "Do you ever sense something evil around the house?" Laughing Water asked.

"One evening the family was watching a movie. During the movie, one of the characters, a well-dressed, rich, sophisticated man transformed into his true being—a gargoyle. At nearly the same instant, Freta started barking and barking at the wall where the coats hung. Her hair was standing straight up." Snow went on explaining. "I never heard her growl and act the way she did that night. I know she was seeing something in another dimension. I also knew it could not have been a Sasquatch, because she never seems frightened or alarmed when she sees them. Whatever she was seeing had to be evil," Snow explained.

"Since it has come so close to you, I must explain what we saw in the silo," Laughing Water said. "There is a being with red eyes and a toadlike back, all bumpy, that has been living there for some time, maybe a couple years. It is feeding off your family's energy. You are a good family with much energy and light to

Diagram I

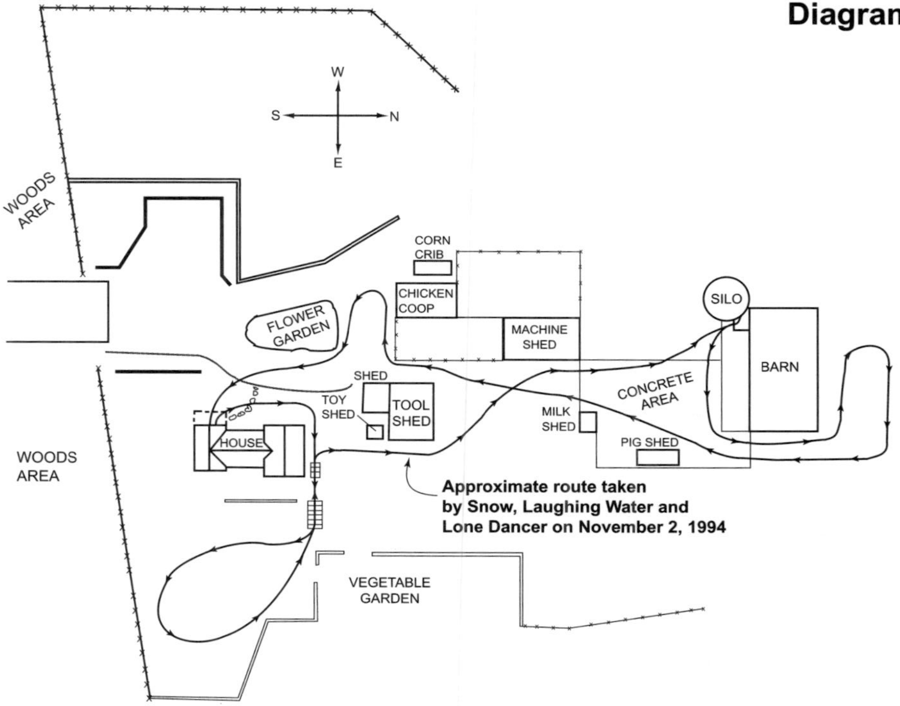

WOODS AREA

FLOWER GARDEN

CORN CRIB

CHICKEN COOP

MACHINE SHED

SHED

TOY SHED

TOOL SHED

HOUSE

SILO

BARN

CONCRETE AREA

PIG SHED

MILK SHED

VEGETABLE GARDEN

WOODS AREA

N
W   E
S

Approximate route taken by Snow, Laughing Water and Lone Dancer on November 2, 1994

share. Evil always looks for people with much energy to fuel itself, leaving you drained and it re-energized. This is a trademark of evil, to only take. As you continually align your will to God's will, you are becoming a more powerful light bearer. Evil will always try to find ways to stop the light from growing in the world," Laughing Water explained.

"Surround yourself in golden white light before entering sleep. If you feel evil lurking nearby, say the words 'I claim the blood of Jesus Christ.' Evil cannot stand in the power and light of these words. Do not be afraid, just know how to protect yourself. As long as beings have free will, there will be many who choose to do evil." Laughing Water continued.

"Is that being in the silo like a gargoyle?" asked Snow.

"Exactly," Laughing Water quickly replied. "I will make a dream catcher for both Arthur and Elden. This will help protect them while they sleep."

They all hugged and said good-bye as if they had known each other for years.

Chapter 5

IT WOULD BE THROUGH A SERIES of dreams starting in November 1994 that much of our true nature would be revealed. We not only came to Snow in her dreams, but to Elden and Arthur's dreams as well. During the next two months, each of them would awaken with more information that answered their questions.

The morning of November 4, Kunta came to give Snow an important message. When Snow awoke, she remembered and interpreted her dream correctly. In the dream she was standing inside a pagoda. It stood in the same place where her house stands. She was standing inside while Kunta was walking outside next to a cornfield. They looked at each other and Snow came running out, so happy to see him. There was a very loving embrace and much joy in their hearts. Snow then took Kunta by the hand and they walked together into her pagoda. While inside, much love and intimacy was expressed.

This was the first dream of Snow's in which so much closeness and physicalness was expressed. When Snow verbalized the dream to Yence in the morning, a certain special card used for divination immediately came to her mind.

She quickly went to get the card, looked at the picture, and read the explanation on it. The card represented Creativity and had an open air pagoda symbolizing the creative self. Snow instantly thought of Kunta and herself walking into her pagoda. Snow interpreted the dream to mean that we Sasquatch are the source of her creativity, her future writing. Also, that we are one with her in expressing our story through her. From our hearts to her heart, to the heart of mother Earth, it will be heard. Snow gave us permission to channel our story and we have chosen her to do so.

On the morning of November 13, Snow awoke remembering another dream. In it, one of our adolescent male Sasquatches poked his head out from behind a tree while Snow was in her car, ready to leave the house.

Before she started the car, Snow looked at the woods in front of her as she had done many times before. She was a little fearful of seeing this Sasquatch and started rolling up her driver's side window as he came around the back of her car. The window was almost closed when he appeared at the door and began to smile. Snow smiled back and all fear melted away.

He opened her door, picked her up, and carried her away toward a field. He jumped over a wire fence with the greatest of ease. Snow understood this dream to mean that she is over the fence regarding any fears about our physical appearance, and that she is willing to go along with us.

On November 30, Kunta came to Elden in a dream. It was time to let the family know that we are also very playful beings. In Elden's dream, he was standing beside the house looking east, toward the back yard. There, he saw Kunta walking out from the woods. "Elden!" Kunta called out in English. Kunta walked into the house with Elden to play for a while. Then they went outside to play in the front yard.

Arthur came walking up the road to the house. Kunta and Elden knew that Arthur was still fearful about our physical appearance, so Elden took Kunta by the hand and led him to the tool shed to hide.

It would take Arthur a long time to become comfortable with seeing us in the physical. Before we became guardians to the family, a great deal of fear had been placed in his mind by beings that are not of light. We will not appear to any of the family members in their waking state until we sense no fear within them.

On December 6, Kunta came to Arthur in a dream. Kunta was crouched down in the back yard, digging a hole and placing a stone in it. Kunta looked at the house and saw Arthur watching. Little by little the fear in Arthur will diminish.

On December 15, Kunta once again came to Elden in a dream. In the dream, Elden remembered that Snow, Elden, and Arthur were about to leave the farm in their car. As they were leaving the driveway, Elden saw a Sasquatch with long muddy hair standing on the side of the road in the woods. They all

Corn Cob Catch

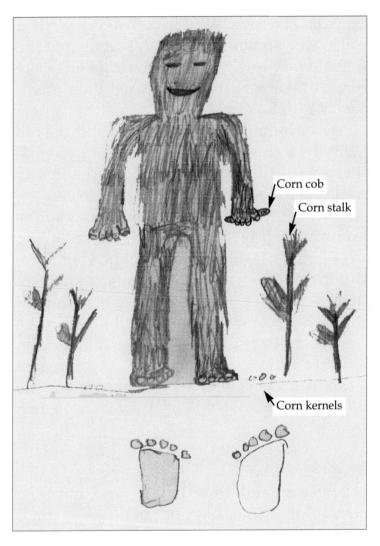

Sasquatch in the corn, by Elden, age 7

drove on and were about to turn a corner when Elden saw another Sasquatch standing at the roadside. It was Kunta, throwing kernels of corn at their car and trying to get their attention, which he did.

Everyone got out of the car and played corncob catch with him. They all laughed and had a good time. After the game, the family returned to the car and came home.

When they got home, they saw two adults and one young Bigfoot walking from the woods and heading north. By showing them this dream, we wanted the family to know we have a good sense of humor. We also wanted to let them know that we could dig into the flesh of the Earth herself, getting muddy hair. Another message is that we do many things as a family unit. That is another reason why we like this family so much—they spend much time together.

On December 20, we telepathically encouraged Snow to consult her medicine cards. She got the hint and drew the Fox card, meaning camouflage. She read the card several times over the next few days. She quickly saw the message we were trying to tell her through the medicine of this animal. The fox is a master of camouflage, as are we. The woodlands with foliage offer lots of medicine protection. The fox teaches you to be like the wind, which is unseen and able to weave through any location or situation. These qualities of fox medicine depict many of our own characteristics. We wanted Snow's choice of this card to help prepare her for the next dream she would have.

It was Christmas Eve and Snow sat quietly in the living room watching the colored lights of their tree. The boys were already asleep in their room and Yence was sitting in a chair, drifting off. She needed some quiet time alone, some time to think about her Christmas wishes. She didn't have to think long. Her wish was for continuing information and for more communication with us.

Snow thought back to the night of January 5, 1994. Almost a full year had passed. A great deal of knowledge and feeling had been shared with her, and much was yet to come. She would often wonder about the first set of tracks coming from the woods that night. She thought they looked so humanlike, but she knew they were not. In the snow they were shallow and so far apart, one in front of the other. She found no toe prints in the set of tracks that were like the ones she had found in the woods the following day. As she drifted off to sleep, she wondered about this and once again wished her Christmas wish. She knew very well from past experiences that many wishes do come true. Patience was the key.

Early Christmas morning we granted Snow's wish. In a dream, Kunta came to answer her question about the humanlike appearance of that first set of tracks. In the dream, Snow was looking out of her kitchen window toward the back yard. In front of one of the many six-foot-tall evergreen trees in the yard, Kunta stood looking at Snow. He walked to the side of the tree; then he walked in front of it to the other side. Kunta again walked to the front of the tree, where he walked into the tree and disappeared.

After Snow saw Kunta vanish, she saw a man with blond hair standing in front of the same tree. He was dressed from head to toe in a camouflage outfit and wore what appeared to be a camouflage beekeeper's hat on his head. The man's actions were exactly the same as Kunta's. He walked from the front to both sides of the tree before disappearing into it.

It was 6:00 A.M. Christmas morning when the boys woke everyone up to see what was under the Christmas tree. Snow lay in bed for a few minutes repeating the dream verbally to herself and Yence. She did not want her Christmas wish to vanish. She wanted to make sure it was in her conscious mind so she could record it later. Snow felt like a child herself that Christmas morning. What she had wished for came true. She felt very special and honored that we had granted her wish when we did.

Once again she did a fine job interpreting the message from the dream. The man in a camouflage outfit was really Kunta. We not only have the ability to shape-shift into any animal we need to in order to do our work, but we can shape-shift into human beings as well.

Her interpretation made sense and felt right to Snow. She thought of the Qabala and all its levels of consciousness. She mostly thought of the level of Tiphareth and remembered that magic and miracles can take place when tapping into its powers. It was the same level of consciousness that Jesus Christ drew from to perform his miracles of healing. He could turn water into wine and one loaf of bread into many by using this level of consciousness.

The Sasquatch, angels, gnomes, fairies, and thousands of other interdimensional beings are aware of and use the powers that reside within the Qabala—the tree of life, the caduceus, the cross (see Spiritual Road Maps).

Spiritual Road Maps

Different in appearance but similar in content and purpose

Qabala

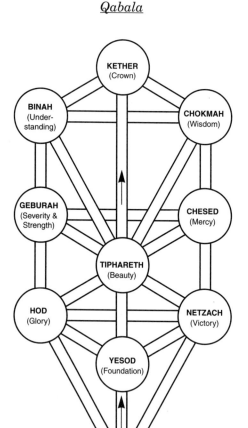

The ten Sephiroth (the ten levels of consciousness) within the map of the tree of life and the titles that reflect the character of the energy found at the level.

Symbol from *Simplified Magic*

Kether—Crown—Pure Light
Tiphareth—Sun— Christ Center— Harmony— Healing
Yesod—Moon—Tides— Astral and Etheric Plane
Malkuth—Earth— Physical Life Kingdom of Man and Woman

By obeying the spiritual and moral laws of purity, unselfishness, honesty, and love, you will gradually ascend the middle path or the straight and narrow (good red road) back to the Great Spirit— (God).

Spiritual Road Maps—*cont'd.*

Different in appearance but similar in content and purpose

Cross

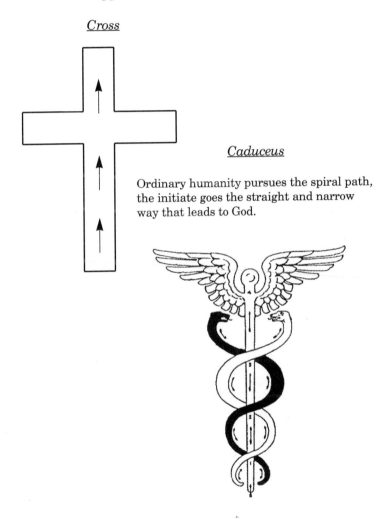

Caduceus

Ordinary humanity pursues the spiral path, the initiate goes the straight and narrow way that leads to God.

The Way of Initiation
Symbol in part from
The Rosicrucian Cosmo-Conception

These levels of consciousness, spheres of various powers, and gifts are for all to use. As always, responsibility comes with knowledge and power.

All beings designed with free will can tap into these powers. Unfortunately many misuse these powers for selfish gain. Remember, nothing anyone does, good or bad, is left unrecorded on the Akaskic records—the external movie reels of our lives.

The law of karma—for every action there is an equal and opposite reaction—is constantly at work. It exists to help you realize your behavior, be it good or bad. All you have to do is be sensitive to what the universe is telling you. God is always talking to you in one way or another to guide you back to your center.

Chapter 6

THE EARTH CHANGES ARE UPON US. The Sasquatch or Bigfoot, as you call us, are only one of many interdimensional beings that will become more visible as these changes occur. We have chosen Snow to be one of our spokespersons to send out the truth about our species and our concerns.

A major concern is, of course, pollution in all its forms. You know what you are doing. You must change your ways now! Human are the only creatures that spoil their own nests. You would think that because you use your rational minds, you would know better. The harm and wrongs you do to your Earth Mother you do to yourself. Fossil fuel is obsolete! You have had the technology for developing solar power or methane as alternate automotive fuels for more than forty years.

Another concern is the unhealthy life styles you choose to lead. Don't you realize that your physical bodies are vehicles for your soul to do its work in? They are two separate things that are united at birth and separated at death. The divine spark (God) cannot work and shine through you when you keep choosing unhealthy behaviors, unhealthy thoughts, unhealthy drugs, and unhealthy foods. It is your job to make yourself fit so God can flow through you to do great works.

Another personal concern is your attitude and desire to capture, or worse, kill one of our kind so you can dissect us or use us as a trophy. If you were spiritually rich, you would not have a need or a desire to do this. It is important that you understand the truth about us. We are beings of great understanding, but we have little hope of being understood. It is a shame that you humans place so much importance upon the physical.

We have been designed by the Great Spirit just as you have been. We are tall and strong with hair that completely covers our bodies, but we are not animals or monsters, as most people think. This may be hard for you to accept, but we are more spiritually and intellectually advanced than humankind. That is the reason you have no physical proof of our existence.

We have knowledge of all the entrances and exits of the portals that exist on Earth. There have been times when our young ones have wandered out of these portals. Sadly, they are often killed and left for dead on roadsides. Their bodies and souls are quickly gathered and brought through a portal to our domain.

We feel the loss of our loved ones just like you humans do. We have shown patience and understanding with the human race when accidents like this have happened. What saddens us is your conscious pursuit and intent to harm us.

We are beings of great gentleness. We do not harm any other species. We eat only greenery, no meat. We are time-jumpers, time-walkers. This means we have the ability to go into the past as well as the future. The portals are involved in this process. Trees are very important to us. They provide protection as camouflage, and more importantly, some even protect the entrances where portals exist. The tree itself is not a portal, but that tree grows where a portal exists. There are many truths in your fairy tales, such as trees being doorways into other dimensions.

Until now, humankind has had little luck seeing us. This is due not only to the fact that we are masters of camouflage, but that we are telepathically aware of your desires and wishes. It saddens us that humankind's mentality is still focused upon wanting to kill or destroy things you do not understand. Your physical world is only the tip of the iceberg. It is time that you become aware of and believe that there are trillions of other lifeforms around you and in space.

A vast, intricate hierarchy of order exists. Each species has its own work, its role to play in the unfolding of the Great Mystery. When any one species becomes extinct, it brings humankind one step closer to their own extinction. This truth applies not only to the species in your physical world, but to the beings that exist around you in other dimensions as well.

We are Earth keepers—healers and protectors of Mother Earth. It is sometimes necessary for us to work in your physical domain. At times we must look through rock piles to find certain stones we need. These stones, with their various frequencies, are used to mend the breaks in the electrical grid patterns surrounding Mother Earth. Some of you have seen us at work doing this. We mostly work by night when we need to be in your physical world. The darkness allows us to work without being seen by humankind.

We also tunnel into the flesh of the Earth herself. A whole other world exists below the Earth's surface. We have been preparing it for those humans who are the "light bearers."

This is a select group of spiritually evolved people who will form the new, spiritually based civilization after all the Earth changes have stopped.

Other people with the right type of high frequency or vibration will be saved by walking through portals into other dimensions. We will be your guides into places of refuge. Please do not be frightened of us. Please do not attempt to kill us! We are here to help you.

Our work has increased tenfold during the last 200 years. We, like other interdimensional beings, are having a hard time keeping up with all the pollution you humans are creating. For some reason you think that there will be no negative repercussions to your insensitive, unwise behaviors. "You reap what you sow," and you are sowing the seeds of devastation in your Earth Mother. We have observed this same behavior for thousands of years. The cycle of history unfortunately repeats itself. The rise and fall of humankind is so predictable. You are now once again at the threshold of technology that existed in the time of Atlantis. Will you repeat the mistakes, the misuse of your technology, as they did, causing their demise? Or will you finally realize that your spirituality should be intimately involved with this power in technology.

The Earth changes are and will continue to occur. There will be many natural disasters that Mother Earth will bring forth. This is a result of what humankind has sown. Isn't it clear to you that what you have sown and continue to sow is not good? You must look at Mother Earth as you would look at a good mother with a disobedient, selfish child. A good mother has to set limits of what is right and wrong. This will not only protect the child, but all others and things around them. So it is with Mother Earth and her children. Action is being taken to protect trillions of innocent lifeforms, both physical and nonphysical, from humankind's selfish, indulgent behaviors.

What are your goals? Money, physical wealth, power? These are not evil in themselves, but they are often used as a test in one's spiritual journey. That's what it really is all about. We are all on a spiritual journey home to our Creator. Come follow us on the straight and narrow that leads to God. Do not be like ordinary humanity, who pursues the spiral path to God.

The Great Spirit has designed us all with free will. We have learned that by aligning our wills to God's, harmony, peace and wisdom abound. There is great joy when a soul knows its purpose in the scheme of things. We have learned through the centuries to take the straight and narrow. It is the most direct route to God.

Look deep within your souls. Your divine spark will light your way.

Sasquatch as drawn by Arthur, age 10

Afterword

OUR RELATIONSHIP WITH SNOW and her family continues. We have revealed more information and insights about our true nature through the continual use of dreams and the sense of smell. New avenues of communication continue to open up. Our next book will share this knowledge.

It is our hope that you will open your minds and hearts and allow yourselves to experience greater realities beyond your physical world. We hope you will view the world and the universe around you from a new perspective.

Appendix A

THERE ARE OTHER PEOPLE outside of my family who have had Sasquatch experiences. Their visits from the Sasquatch took place after I told them about my *Story in the Snow*. I have been guided through dreams to keep a low profile about my relationship with Bigfoot, only sharing my story with those whom I feel are spiritually rich.

The first friend of mine to experience the Sasquatch after hearing my *Story in the Snow* was Laughing Water. It was after Laughing Water and Lone Dancer's first visit to my farm in November of 1994 that Laughing Water actually saw a Bigfoot in the physical. As both of them were driving home, Laughing Water looked out her right window and saw a tall male white Sasquatch standing next to a tree, with his hair blowing in the breeze.

Later that winter, Laughing Water noticed three different sized sets of Bigfoot tracks in the snow outside her apartment. Each set had toe prints and what looked to be the impression of their long hair. Laughing Water asked her son and her husband along with Lone Dancer what they thought had made the tracks. They all believed Bigfoot had made them.

The second friend was visited by the Sasquatch while she was driving home from Madison, Wisconsin. Her whole car smelled like that of a skunk, even though all her windows were closed. This took place a few days after I told her my *Story in the Snow*.

My third friend to have a Sasquatch encounter after hearing my story was Grace. It was on a very snowy Wednesday night, November 20, coming home from puppy obedience classes, when Grace witnessed something very few of us humans are gifted to see.

Grace drove her little car down a desolate, snow-covered country road as her daughter and six-month-old golden retriever were dozing in the back seat. It was just in the matter of a few moments that Grace saw what many would say is impossible.

From the left side of the road appeared a large brown cloud floating over the road. As it got to the center of the road, it changed into what looked like the back half of a huge deer or moose. By the time it moved off the right side of the road, it looked like a wide-shouldered man about six or seven feet tall walking into a field. He had the posture of someone who was cold, head down with arms in front.

Later that same night, as Grace was putting her daughter to bed, they both saw huge boot-type prints in the virgin snow on the sidewalk outside their house. The prints were one in front of the other and far apart. Grace went out to look at them after her daughter went to sleep. They were eighteen inches long and six to seven feet apart. They were a heel-toed boot-print type.

Grace also noticed deer tracks in her front yard. They were strange because they were large and were one in front of the other.

Before that night, Grace and her daughter had been experiencing many horrible nightmares and visits from unseen evil beings. After that night in the snow, there was peace. This is the same type of experience that we had. Before the night the Sasquatch left answers in the snow, many times Arthur woke up delirious with fear. After seeing the Bigfoot tracks, the nightmares stopped.

My spiritually rich friends believe that Sasquatch is a guardian type of being. Grace and I were especially gifted to see the Sasquatch exhibit the ability to shape-shift. Grace viewed it in person. I viewed it in the changing of the footprints in the snow, and through dreams.

Appendix B

There have been several counties in Wisconsin that have reported Bigfoot sightings. All of them have been mentioned in *Sasquatch: The Apes Among Us* by John Green. Following are reports of three of these.

In Monroe County, in the city of Cashton, Wisconsin, a seven-foot creature was seen in the fall of 1976.

A more personal connection to this area came in November of 1996. Two weeks before Thanksgiving, I called my friend who had just moved, with her family, to Cashton, Wisconsin. An interesting point to note here is that this family sold their house to Grace! My friend who knew of my story in the snow informed me that she had just read from the Cashton paper that there had been a recent Bigfoot sighted on Highway 33, very close to where she lives.

In Waupaca County, in the city of Fremont, Wisconsin, there was a group of twelve men on a deer drive on November 30, 1968. Six of the men reported seeing a Bigfoot standing in a marsh. They all reported it as being non-threatening and docile (also printed in an article in *Argosy* magazine).

In Walworth County, near the city of Lake Geneva, Wisconsin, a Bigfoot was seen running across a highway near the Illinois border.

This is also the area where Chief Bigfoot lived with his peaceful tribe called the Pottawatomies. The chief got his name after doing a ceremonial dance in the county. Midway through the dance it began to rain. The chief continued to dance, collecting coats of mud on his feet that made them huge. It is important to note that the Pottawatomies were reported to be docile and affectionate to the early explorers, not at all warlike.

I believe there is some kind of connection between Chief Bigfoot and the Bigfoot species.

Appendix C

SOME AREAS AND PLACES to claim the name of Bigfoot:

1. Bigfoot Beach State Park, Walworth County, south of Lake Geneva, Wisconsin.

2. Bigfoot High School, Walworth County, Lake Geneva, Wisconsin.

3. The town of Bigfoot in Illinois, just south of the Wisconsin/Illinois border on Highway 67.

Publisher's Note

SEVERAL YEARS AGO, I was in the process of constructing crystal wands. These were made with a large, single-terminated quartz crystal, about one inch in diameter, held by a foot-long copper tube and then wrapped in colored leather. I handcrafted these items for sale and for gifts. The quartz crystals were secured in place with silicon, and they required many hours of drying time—at least twenty-four to forty-eight hours. Normally I would leave my projects out on the dining room table during their various stages of construction.

One night I left several nearly finished crystal wands on the table and then went to bed, exhausted but exhilarated by the enjoyment of crafting these high-energy tools. While lying there nearly asleep, in that restful hypnogogic state, I suddenly became aware of someone or something out in the dining room. I was shocked into full wakefulness, strangely half-frightened and half-excited by what I sensed. It was as if I could see perfectly clearly someone standing by the table near the outside wall, looking down and examining my handiwork. Even more astonishing was the image I saw. It was a large, adult-sized, male Bigfoot. He appeared to have brown fur, and was intently and intelligently studying the wands. I didn't think that if I got out bed and physically walked into the dining room I could see this apparition any more clearly than what I was sensing, so, coward that I was, I stayed in bed.

That vision has never left me, and to this day I wonder why this being chose to examine the wands I was making.

A friend of mine who grew up in rural northern Minnesota on the Iron Range had several Bigfoot experiences.

As a young girl, while she was playing outdoors with her siblings or friends, on more than one occasion she would see what she called a "white gorilla" standing by the edge of the woods watching her. No one else seemed to see this being, or else they didn't care. My friend always believed that the "white gorilla" was there to watch over her and protect her, and she did not feel frightened or surprised to see this creature. As she grew older, the watcher from the edge of the woods no longer made itself visible, but this image remains strongly imbedded in her memory to this day.

—PHYLLIS JEAN GALDE

Bibliography

BOOKS

Andrews, Ted. *Simplified Magic: A Beginners Guide to the New Age Qabala.* St. Paul, Minn.: Llewellyn Publications, 1989.

Heindel, Max. *The Rosicucian Cosmo-Conception, or Mystic Christianity.* Oceanside, Calif.: The Rosicrucian Fellowship, 1937.

CARDS

Sams, Jamie, and David Carson. *Medicine Cards.* Bear & Co. Used by permission.

To order additional copies of this book,
please send full amount plus $4.00 for
postage and handling for the first book and
50¢ for each additional book.

Send orders to:

GALDE PRESS, INC.
PO Box 460
Lakeville, Minnesota 55044–0460

Credit card orders call 1–800–777–3454

Write for our free catalog.